The Odd S~~~

BOOK FOR BLOKES

JIGGLE!

CLICK!

by Allan Plenderleith

RAVETTE PUBLISHING

For Dad

The Odd Squad and all related characters © 2009
Created by Allan Plenderleith
www.allanplenderleith.com

First published in 2009 by
Ravette Publishing Limited

ISBN: 978-1-84161-319-2

May the farts be with you...always.

At work, make sure your secretary
backs up her stuff on a floppy.

Never ask a woman to shave her beaver.

When cuddling up naked by a fireplace,
beware of stray sparks.

Whilst perusing internet porn at work
be careful not to get caught.

How to get out of annoying
games of charades.

When suffering from the cold,
always make the most of it.

Always keep your condoms
away from the vicinity of goldfish.

Never take too many laxatives.

How to get a woman to fall in love with you – buy a cream doughnut.

Never hang a dartboard near
an open window.

Show your woman you love her –
buy her something with diamonds.

Never be afraid to ask for directions.

On long journeys, remember to let the dog get some fresh air.

If your lady begins tickling your bum
during sex, just relax and enjoy it.

Never try to smuggle some dope through customs.

When picking your nose, never go too deep.

Never visit your nan the night after
a fancy dress party.

How to make a cat flap.

Remember – always eat 5 portions
of veg a day.

During oral sex, beware of the gag reflex.

On sea journeys, always remember the flares.

How to tell if your cat is a chick.

Give your lady something different
– a golden shower.

During golf, make sure your ball never lands in a bit of rough.

Never give a woman wearing a g-string a wedgie.

At the weekend, why not hang out
with your mates down the pub.

Need a wee during a car journey?
Simply find a nearby lay-by.

Itchy bum in public? Too embarrassed to scratch? Simply find a fire hydrant.

Whilst out sailing, always be
alert for icebergs.

For fun whilst out clubbing, try playing
the Spot the Camel Toe game.

Beware of women who use cunning tricks to get you to do the housework.

When playing with yourself,
always remember to lock the door.

When the missus asks you to bring home a juicy pear from the market, take advantage of her blunder.

To make round-buying simpler,
put your money in a kitty.

Remember, the length of a Valentine card is directly related to the size of your penis.

Beware of sexual encounters with older ladies.

To experience a fun, free, spinning vortex simply stand between two old ladies.

Give your lady a treat – spend the weekend deep inside her bush.

On cold days, try playing
Spot the Old Lady's Nipples game.

Never give a dog mouth to mouth.

Never trust a woman who says
she wants a threesome.

Remember – women love a good muff diver.

Always speak clearly when asking someone to check out your new spectacles.

Never twiddle a woman's nipples too much.

The upside of getting a job at a nuclear power plant.

Beware of people coming round collecting for the old folks' home.

Fed up with chips? Try onion rings.

Stay away from coffee machines
which are out of order.

Unfortunately, sex is not possible
when she has the painters in.

Never go searching for Christmas presents
in your parents' bedroom.

Beware of slightly deaf chip shop staff.

Never tell a lady you're going to give her a pearl necklace for her birthday.

Always go for a pee before making love.

Never clean your ear with a pencil
near a doorway.

Why you should always ban pets
from the bedroom.

What happens when a woman moves
in with you.

When peeing in a phone box,
make sure it's just a quicky.

How to spot someone having phone sex.

When buying a new mobile,
opt for the poo as you go plan.

One of the few benefits of a
poo that won't break off.

The perils of the old 'hole in the bottom of the popcorn' trick.

How to make potato wedgies.

To brighten up the weekend, simply
glue a pound coin onto the pavement.

How to stop your flatmates nicking your food.

There's one place no-one will touch
your beloved remote control.

Never use cooking oil instead of suntan oil.

How to make sure you never get
socks for Christmas.

After a big curry it's best to
take precautions.

How to castrate a cat – the easy way.

When answering the front door in your dressing gown, be careful you don't have a semi.

Never trust a woman who uses sex toys.

Why your woman should never sneeze
during oral sex.

Women love waking up on their birthday to a large, sparkling ring.

Remember – women love something
hard in bed.